# Excellence
# in
# Upper-Level Writing
# 2019/2020

**The Gayle Morris
Sweetland Center for Writing**

Edited by
Dana Nichols

Published in 2020 by Michigan Publishing
University of Michigan Library

© 2020 Gayle Morris Sweetland Center for Writing

Permission is required to reproduce material from this title in other
publications, coursepacks, electronic products, and other media.

Please send permission requests to:

Michigan Publishing
1210 Buhr Building
839 Greene Street
Ann Arbor, MI 48104
lib.pod@umich.edu

ISBN 978-1-60785-583-5

# Table of Contents
*Excellence in Upper-Level Writing*

Winners list                                                                      5

Nominees list                                                                     6

Introduction                                                                      9


**Prize for Excellence in Upper-Level Writing**
**(Sciences)**

Cerebral Organoids: Promising New Window into Neurodevelopment       11

Gene editing for the 21st century: CRISPR/Cas9 and Prime Editing      27


**Prize for Excellence in Upper-Level Writing**
**(Social Sciences)**

D.C. Dog Fight:  Principle and Pragmatism of the Bush-era Supreme Court   37

The Plastic Problem: What are Scientists doing to Reduce their            43
   Environmental Footprint?


**Prize for Excellence in Upper-Level Writing**
**(Humanities)**

عنوان                                                                             49

A Second Exile: Mario Benedetti's Absence in English                     59

# Excellence in Upper-Level Writing 2019/2020

**Sweetland Writing Prize Chair**

Dana Nichols

**Sweetland Writing Prize Committee**

Angie Berkley

Jimmy Brancho

Gina Brandolino

Raymond McDaniel

Carol Tell

**Sweetland Writing Prize Judges**

Anna Cornell

Gina Cervetti

Kim Hess

Benjamin Hollenbach

Tugce Kayaal

Jane Kitaevich

Hongling Lu

Christine Modey

Ragnhild Nordaas

Lucy Peterson

Colleen Seifert

Twila Tardif

Niku Tarhechu Tarhesi

**Administrative Support**

Laura Schulyer

Aaron Valdez

# Winners List

## Excellence in Upper-Level Writing (Sciences)

**Alice Sorel**, "Cerebral Organoids: Promising New Window into
  Neurodevelopment"
*Nominated by Jimmy Brancho, WRITING 400: Writing and Research in the Sciences*

**Franco Tavella**, "Gene editing for the 21st century: CRISPR/Cas9 and
  Prime Editing"
*Nominated by Qiong Yang, BIOPHYS 450/550: Intro to Biophysics Laboratory*

## Excellence in Upper-Level Writing (Social Sciences)

**Max Steinbaum**, "D.C. Dog Fight: Principle and Pragmatism of the Bush-era
  Supreme Court"
*Nominated by Jacob Walden, POLSCI 319: Politics of Civil Liberties and Civil Rights*

**Maryellen Zbrozek**, "The Plastic Problem: What are Scientists doing to Reduce
  their Environmental Footprint?"
*Nominated by Julie Halpert, ENVIRON 320: Environmental Journalism -
  Reporting about Science, Policy and Public Health*

## Excellence in Upper-Level Writing (Humanities)

**Jinan Abufarha**, "عنوان"
*Nominated by Christine Modey, WRITING 300: Seminar in Peer
  Writing Consultation*

**Davis Boos**, "A Second Exile: Mario Benedetti's Absence in English"
*Nominated by Marlon James Sales, COMPLIT 322: Translated Wor(l)ds*

# Nominees List

| Student | Instructor |
|---------|------------|
| Jinan Abufarha | Christine Modey |
| Theresa Benton | Emilia Askari |
| Karis Blaker | June Howard |
| Davis Boos | Marlon James Sales |
| Sam Braden | Christine Modey |
| Kate Brantley | Rosie Sharp |
| William Chown | Omolade Adunbi |
| Arabella Delgado | June Howard |
| Matteo Dristas | Ben Hansen |
| Annabelle Farkas | Sara Morell |
| Lauren Florsheim | Meaghan Pearson |
| Emily Furstenberg | Angie Berkley |
| Gillian Graham | Erin McAuliffe |
| Anooshka Gupta | Jesse Yeh |
| Jiaheng He | Hui Deng |
| Minjun Jin | Qiong Yang |
| Josh Johr | Mark Kligerman |
| John Dorigo Jones | Hui Deng |
| Seth Kattapong-Graber | Jimmy Brancho |
| Dahlia Katz | Mary Grace Pellegrini |
| Lauren Levitt | Marlon James Sales |
| Douillet Margot | Gabriel VanLoozen |
| Natalie McMyn | Emilia Askari |
| Solomon Medintz | Elizabeth Anderson |
| Hannah Meloche | San Duanmu |
| Lucas Merritt | Mary Hennessy |
| Samantha Nelson | David Gold |
| Preet Patel | Michael Meyer |
| Anshul Vinod Puli | San Duanmu |

| Student | Instructor |
| --- | --- |
| Aravinth Ravitha | Meaghan Pearso |
| Lynnitaane Riley | Jesse Yeh |
| Jordan Schuler | Mary Grace Pellegrini |
| Emily Shimroth | Omolade Adunbi |
| Maria Sobrino | Mary Hennessy |
| Alice Sorel | Jimmy Brancho |
| Max Steinbaum | Jacob Walden |
| Brandon Stras | Sara Morell |
| Franco Tavella | Qiong Yang |
| Justin Vorhees | Cody Walker |
| Rebecca Yi | Erin McAuliffe |
| Hanna Zaretsky | Gabriel VanLoozen |
| Maryellen Zbrozek | Julie Halpert |
| Jialin Zhang | RosieSharp |
| Gerstle Zoe | Julie Halpert |

# Introduction

All undergraduates who have graduated from the College of Literature, Science and the Arts since the late 1970s have taken at least one upper-level writing course. Such courses are offered by approximately 35 departments every semester—in the humanities, social sciences, and sciences. These courses challenge students to produce complex, evidence-based arguments; to improve their writing by responding to feedback from their peers and instructors; to develop effective revision strategies; and to refine their ability to write within and beyond the disciplines in which they major. Students encounter a variety of writing assignments in diverse disciplinary genres: from lab reports to personal memoirs. They may adapt their arguments for distinct audiences (readers of a popular science journal as well as specialists in biology). The writing included in this volume represents some of the best work produced by students in upper-level writing courses during the past year.

The Sweetland Fellows Seminar participants read all the submissions for the upper-level writing prize and chose the essays that appear in these pages. These are difficult choices, for instructors from 18 departments nominated an impressive body of writing. All of the essays submitted were well written, convincing, and engaging. Those selected for this volume earned particular admiration for their remarkable qualities. Each prize-winning student develops original arguments about complex and difficult topics, demonstrates precision in word choice and sentence structure, and draws the reader along to compelling conclusions. Each essay in this volume witnesses to the vibrant intellectual life of the University. Each speaks to how much students can contribute to our knowledge of the world we inhabit.

I thank the seminar fellows for their thoughtful work rating the essay submissions: Anna Cornell (Classical Languages and Literatures), Gina

Cervetti (School of Education), Kim Hess (Sociology), Benjamin Hollenbach (Anthropology), Tugce Kayaal (Near Eastern Studies), Jane Kitaevich (Political Science), Hongling Lu (Material Science and Engineering), Christine Modey (Sweetland), Ragnhild Nordaas (Political Science), Lucy Peterson (Political Science), Colleen Seifert (Psychology), Twila Tardif (Psychology), and Niku Tarhechu Tarhesi (Anthropology). Much gratitude is also owed to Aaron Valdez, who designed this book; Laura Schuyler, who coordinated the submission and judging process); and, especially, to Dana Nichols, who edited the collection. Finally, thank you to the students and instructors who strive for excellence in writing, whether or not they get prizes for their efforts. Good writing is always worthwhile!

*Theresa Tinkle*
Sweetland Center for Writing

# Excellence in Upper-Level Writing (Sciences)

## Cerebral Organoids: Promising New Window into Neurodevelopment
by Alice Sorel

*From WRITING 400: Writing and Research in the Sciences*
*Nominated by Jimmy Brancho*

A scientific literature review is expected to provide a perspective on the history of a field and to update readers on its most recent developments. Alice's review of a neuroscientific advancement in cerebral organoids accomplishes that handily and with surprising rigor. But Alice's essay stands out for its personality, poetry, and liveliness. The review locates the science not in an inorganic and detached way, but always from the perspectives of the humans conducting the work, hoping for its successful application, searching always for answers. She is playful at times, breaking the reader out of the lab and into the library or even their own kitchens. Lastly, Alice's intricate prose features wonderfully varied sentence structure. She doesn't just convey information. She sits the reader down and invites them to wonder along with her at the challenge, ingenuity, and potential of science.

*-- Jimmy Brancho*

# Cerebral Organoids:
# Promising New Window into Neurodevelopment

It is not birth, marriage, or death, but gastrulation, which is truly the most important time in your life.

*Lewis Wolpert*

## Abstract

The pressing need for *in vitro* models to investigate neurodevelopment is ignited by the complexity of the human brain. Cerebral organoids, grown from human pluripotent stem cells reprogrammed in a way that allows them to self-organize and develop in a manner that resembles the human brain development, recently have been the topic of heated debates and discussions in the field of neuroscience. These three-dimensional clumps of cells provide us with an unprecedented opportunity to recapitulate the molecular features of neurodevelopment that can't be analyzed in any other existing model. This technique already granted researchers remarkable insights about neurological disorders that were inaccessible for studying before due to species-specific differences. While theoretically cerebral organoids hold a great deal of promise to become the golden standard in neuroscience, there are still many problems connected with using this tool today. This literature review is focused on the advantages, applications, and challenges of human brain organoids as *in vitro* models for studying neurodevelopment and its disorders. The necessary improvement of the protocol and progress in the overall understanding of this relatively new system will increase the complexity of phenotypes that can be modeled by using it and will continue to revolutionize the field.

## Introduction

The main goal of neuroscience, in all its multidisciplinary and technologically advanced glory, essentially is to understand how and why the brain is formed in this very specific manner. Conveniently enough, neural development across the different species of vertebrates is highly conserved, which means that it is sufficiently similar to reveal universal and fundamental processes. While the previous research using animal models (mice, chickens, non-human primates) provided invaluable insights into the nature of cellular and molecular mechanisms underlying the formation of the brain and central nervous system, there are still many species-specific features left unexplored. However, in the case with the human brain, struggles with research in this area are closely connected with difficulties in obtaining adequate tissue samples and a plethora of ethical issues. Consequently, we have the following situation: even though we need to understand the process of brain formation in humans and narrow down the nature of its dysfunctions, we also have very limited resources to do so, due to multiple reasons.

This is where scientific progress comes to the rescue: recent advancement in the field presents a technique that permits the creation of stem-cell-derived cerebral organoids. These models serve as an invaluable tool to help us understand the mechanisms of human brain development *in vitro*. They provide an unprecedented opportunity to recapitulate the unique features of the brain development that is specific to our species in a complex tissue-like environment, allowing us to investigate the nature of our cognitive origin. In this literature review, I want to focus on the promises and challenges that cerebral organoid pose and evaluate if this method can become the most adequate model for studying the brain development in mammals overall and humans specifically. I will start by explaining the details of this technique, which is the first aim of a given piece. The second goal is to put cerebral organoids in perspective: by providing a historical tour of how discoveries about the brain and its formation were made using cell culture and animal models, I will explain a context that underlies a need for new tools. The third aim is to describe possible applications of organoids, which increases their appeal for both researchers and the general population. Lastly, I will go over drawbacks and challenges this model poses, and possible ways of addressing them in the future.

Before delving deep into technical details, promising results and possible shortcomings of this tool that *Nature* has chosen as "Method of the Year 2017", seems reasonable to explain it first. Organoids are defined as three-dimensional spheroids made from stem cells; they recapitulate the main characteristics of specific organs and provide a valuable opportunity to study their development. As Andrews and Nowakowski explain in their most current review of cerebral organoids, work that revolutionized the field, pioneered this technique and identified how three-dimensional organoids are viewed comes from the labs of Yoshiki Sasai (Eiraku et al., 2008, Kadoshima et al., 2013) and Juergen Knoblich (Lancaster et al., 2013). These researchers have demonstrated the ability of stem cells to self-organize in a manner that resembles structural features of the developing human brain, including the reproduction of major cell classes. This breakthrough turned cerebral organoids into an experimentally tractable model that allows investigating the details of the human brain and central nervous system formation that can't be seen in existing animal models due to species-specific differences.

Cerebral organoids are essentially made up of human-derived pluripotent cells, for example, induced pluripotent or embryonic stem cells. They are suspended in media that have components necessary for neural induction and differentiation. According to Kelava and Lancaster (2016), "embedding cells in a supportive extracellular matrix gel, called Matrigel, provided the 3D context for the self-organization of these cells into organized epithelia with typical apicobasal polarity." After letting cerebral organoids to differentiate and grow in static culture for several weeks, they are placed in orbital shakers or spinning bioreactors (Qian et al., 2016) to promote better distribution of media and let oxygen reach the center of the organoids. After that, organoids (that can reach up to 4-5 mm in diameter) are kept in suspension for as long as needed. During several months, over various time points, they can be evaluated to provide insights into neurodevelopmental processes and model neural disease (Andrews and Nowakowski, 2019). One of the most remarkable features of cerebral organoids is described by Kelava and

Lancaster in their review of the protocol for this technique: they point out not only continuous brain lobes but also cavities that are filled with fluid, exactly like ventricles in the brain.

Looking back at the history of major discoveries that create the foundation of neuroscience today stimulates both critical analysis of the gaps in our knowledge and appreciation of the new models that are trying to bridge them. By putting cerebral organoids in the broader context, it is easier to see the value of this new and promising technique while also addressing its limitations and aspects of the protocol that still leave much to be desired.

## History of Neurodevelopmental Models
### Neural Cell Cultures

Scientists' attempts to study the development of the brain and the nervous system began more than a century ago. The father of the first artificial cell culture, Ross Granville Harrison, in 1907 demonstrated the way to isolate neurons from the brains (adult and fetal) and cultivate them *in vitro*. Even prior to that work, in 1889, Wilhelm His Sr. observed what will be known in the future as neural stem cells (NSCs). He made a discovery that helped establish neuronal doctrine: that neurons in the human cortex migrate to the outer surface from ventricular zones, where they are born (Kelava and Lancaster, 2016). Pasko Rakic, who almost single-handedly pioneered the research of the formation and evolution of the cerebral cortex, named those cells radial glia in 2003 (Rakic, 2003). Rakic discovered that basal processes of radial glial cells allow neurons to migrate into their final positions, using them as scaffolds. Radial glia were established as the source of neurons and glia in the developing brain of mammals about 20 years ago.

The first culture of isolated NSCs was created in 1989 by Dr. Sally Temple (Temple, 1989). This work was a starting point for stem cell research in the brain, which led to a pivotal discovery. NSCs were realized to have a great promise as a technique for basic research as well as a therapeutic model to provide insights into neurodevelopmental issues because of their potential for creating multiple types of neurons. However, they are not the most appropriate for studying the development of the brain *in vivo* since isolated NSCs in culture are not able to recapitulate the entire range of neural lineages. This created a pressing need for a more viable model that offers more promising perspectives for research, and scientists turned their attention to live organisms that naturally go through the process of neurogenesis and brain formation.

*Animal Models*

Perhaps, the most common model for understanding mammalian brain development can be found in multiple homes up to this day. *Mus musculus*, usually known as a common or house mouse, became a golden standard in neuroscience in the last 50 years. This popularity is explained easily: mice are convenient to study because they recapitulate enough of the features of human-specific brain formation, are relatively easy to maintain in the laboratory settings, and, most of all, they offer a great range for genetic manipulation, inactivating (knocking out) or adding (knocking in) genes to accommodate multiple research goals. Most, if not all, of our current insights into the function of genes that are essential for proper neurodevelopment and genes that contribute to the origin of neurodevelopmental disorders, comes from research done using mouse models.

Talking about conveniently preserved across the species similarities is easy when data suggests extrapolation to some extent. The problem arises when differences in the process of neurodevelopment become irreconcilable. Notably, the cell cycle in NCSs, which plays a critical role in neurogenesis, lasts much longer in humans than in mice. Moreover, humans demonstrate a bigger diversity of neuronal types. Then, of course, there is a problem of the size and gyrencephalic nature of the human brain versus a smooth, lissencephalic, surface on the mouse brain.

While mice do not provide a model that recapitulates human brain development the most accurately (for obvious reasons, since mice are not humans and vice versa), Marshal and Mason (2019) raise many interesting points in their paper. They argue that mice should not be entirely disregarded even in the light of such a promising new tool as cerebral organoids from human-derived pluripotent stem cells. Given how much *in vivo* data on mouse brain development exists already, collected through decades of research performed using mouse models, it would be unreasonable to abandon it altogether. These data, plus comprehensive descriptions of mutant phenotypes give us today an ability to compare and validate cerebral organoids as an appropriate model for neurodevelopment (Marshal and Mason, 2019). Furthermore, organoids, even if grown from mouse-derived stem cells, can potentially replace mouse models or at least significantly reduce the numbers of animals used the brain development research across the globe. The authors also provide a summary of the most important advantages and disadvantages of organoids created using mouse or human stem cells, and those are surprisingly similar. In addition, they argue that some of the limitations of organoids can be overcome by using mice, where they will be an intermediate step between current models that have their problems and "fully developed", improved organoids of the future.

## Applications of Cerebral Organoids

### Neurodevelopmental Disorders

Most of the knowledge we have today about embryonic development was gathered by extrapolating from animal models to human biology. To truly understand ourselves, the nature of our extraordinary cognitive evolution, we must use tools that can offer more, tools that are relevant and applicable to our species because they are based on our cells. Thus far, cerebral organoids fill this need. For example, Lancaster et al. (2013) document a novel method of studying human neurodevelopmental processes and recreating features of neurodevelopmental disorders that can't be demonstrated in different models. To do so, researchers grew *in vitro* culture of cerebral organoids from human pluripotent stem cells. The most promising part about this approach is that it recreates fundamental processes of mammalian neurodevelopment as well as characteristics of human brain development.

Authors see the application of this technique as a model for researching a variety of neurodevelopmental processes and disorders that they underlie. The researchers tried to model some aspects of microcephaly in those organoids, eliminating one of the major problems that exist when this condition is recreated in the mouse model. Due to the difference in the rates of expansion of neural progenitor cells before the onset of neurogenesis, mouse models used prior couldn't illustrate the severity of microcephaly seen in humans. Recreating those fine-tuned details and differences in neurodevelopment provides an extremely valuable perspective for neuroscience overall, and this is definitely a very promising application of this technique.

*Evolution*

Pollen et al. (2019) found a different application for cerebral organoids and took a refreshing evolutionary approach. The authors of this dense study created pluripotent stem cell-derived cerebral organoids from a chimpanzee, our closest living relative, to identify human-specific features of brain development, obviously focusing on the cerebral cortex. Their results are fascinating: despite metabolic differences (elevated metabolic stress), models of cerebral organoids preserve gene regulatory networks that regulate primary cell types and developmental processes. Moreover, this study adds to a new field of "cellular anthropology" (Prescott et al., 2015) since, by using cerebral organoids, scientists create a comparative platform for systematic description of the unique molecular features underlying human cortical development and evolution. This analysis of the dissimilarities between human and macaque species that emerged along our lineage in the last six million years using human and chimpanzee cerebral organoid models gives us an unprecedented perspective into patterns of early brain development.

*Therapeutic tools*

Stem cell research has been invigorating multiple areas of biological sciences, from bioengineering to cancer therapies, for several decades. Not surprisingly that organoids are often discussed in the context of their possible application as therapeutic tools in disease-modeling, drug discovery, and transplantation. Conceptually, stem cell research is fueled by the idea that a way to grasp complex biological phenomenon is through an emergent property of multiple structural dynamics. Those dynamics occur due to relatively straightforward local interactions: cell-cell, tissue-tissue. (Sasai, 2013)

Sasai (2013) predicts *in vitro* approaches that are created with the use of self-organizing stem cell culture will yield critical information regarding "dynamic local interactions during emergent organogenesis, in a complementary manner to *in vivo* study". Thus, Lou and Leung (2018) propose that cerebral organoids can be used to mimic the complex cellular heterogeneity of tissues, improve upon existing procedures of drug testing, improving their safety, efficacy, and cost-effectiveness, and also to meet the demands for human tissues for the purpose of transplantation.

*Replacing existing animal models?*

The given question remains open until shortcomings of this technique are addressed; it is possible in theory, while in practice there are still too many obstacles connected with all the factors that are described in the following part of this review. While Marshal and Mason argue that organoids (both mouse and human) can replace mouse models altogether, other researchers voice more cautious predictions and want to supplement animal models with organoids. This would allow to validate both systems and provide a more detailed analysis.

For example, Di Lullo and Kriegstein (2017) propose to investigate with this tool the mechanisms underlying gyrification and human cortical expansion. They stress the importance of human brain organoids for modeling human-specific traits, such as the cell types and structural features of neurodevelopment, or detrimental mutations that are proven to cause various diseases and are difficult to recapitulate in the mouse model.

A recent success was achieved by using cerebral organoids to explore the cellular basis of Miller–Dieker syndrome (MDS), a severe congenital form of lissencephaly (smooth brain). Before for the purpose of studying lissencephaly mouse models were used, however, this compromises the entire research since mice are naturally lissencephalic. Di Lullo and Kriegstein (2017) suggest that relevant cell types or developmental programs that are essential for answering many questions about this and similar disorders can be found in cerebral organoids. Induced pluripotent stem cells derived from patients with MDS were used to create organoids, which demonstrated several developmental phenotypes that are also seen in lissencephaly mouse models (this includes defects in neuronal migration and dysregulation of the neuroepithelial stem cell mitotic spindle).

While overall cerebral organoids offer multiple advantages over mouse models and have a potential to become the golden standard of the neuroscience research in the future, replacing animal-based research or limiting it to only harvesting stem cells, there are still many areas for improvement that are required for this scenario to come true. Admittedly, looking at the bigger picture, it does seem like the next logical step to take, to move from extrapolating from animal models to studying actual human biology using human-derived cells.

## Limitations and Challenges

### Biological

Despite the aforementioned successes and unique information gathered through the use of brain organoids, a model in its early phase of development, current protocol still has many areas for improvement. Di Lullo and Kriegstein (2017) point out a number of limitations, including low reproducibility, incomplete cell type diversity and slow maturation. Another complication is concerned with the inadequate supply of oxygen and nutrients to the central regions of the tissue.

The paper by Quadrato et al. (2016) raises a different issue: there is an urgent need to map the cellular composition and the diversity of cell types present within the various 3D systems. Single-gene markers helped to identify the nature of some cells, yet it is not sufficient to critically examine the potential applications of organoids as model systems, especially for modeling and investigating neuropsychiatric disorders. Immunohistochemistry that is routinely used to distinguish among the various types of cells might not serve its purpose in the case with cerebral organoids, mainly because of inconsistent neuroanatomy and cytoarchitectural patterns. Moreover, the analysis of single-marker genes cannot usually help to conclusively identify cell types. Altered interactions among different cell types from multiple brain regions pose another problem that scientists are yet to tackle.

*Ethical Considerations*

Stem cell research used to be and still is a rather controversial topic in terms of moral and ethical considerations and constraints. It would not come as a surprise that stem cell research to recreate brain organoids propels discussions about limits to what is permissible. While it might be slightly premature to consider consciousness in cerebral organoids that are five millimeters in diameter, there are some recent studies that move forward the conversation regarding the ethics of organoids research in general and cerebral organoids in particular. For example, Trujillo et al. (2019) created human cerebral organoids that actually changed their cellular identity during maturation and showed consistently increased electrical activity over the span of several months. Moreover, neural oscillations in their brain organoids became more complex. Upon reading about this, I couldn't help but wonder if more complex neural oscillations correlate with a more "developed" brain.

In the other study, Luo et al. (2016) discovered disturbingly many similarities in terms of epigenomic signatures of fetal brain development and development of brain organoid. While these achievements can undoubtedly be described as a success and promising future application of this technology, there might be more to consider, especially in terms of ethical repercussions of this kind of research. While moral and ethical considerations must play a role in scientific progress, there is also a fragile balance between speculating about unobtainable and unforeseeable future and critically analyzing the current state of affairs while trying to plan a few steps ahead. Therefore, I feel that while it is appropriate to mention gray areas of research, executive decisions should be made by people with expertise and hopefully a desire to find a compromise that will be the most beneficial for the sake of science and society.

## Conclusion and Future Directions

Neuroscience is relatively young as an academic discipline, and there is always seem to be more questions than answers, which keep scientists guessing and moving forward tirelessly. The emergence of such a potent tool as cerebral organoids that provide a unique chance to recapitulate human brain formation, something unheard of just a decade ago, makes being in the field and observing its development particularly exciting. Due to organoids' capabilities of self-organization, differentiation, and forming complex, biologically relevant and species-specific structures, they are seen as ideal *in vitro* models of neurodevelopment, disease pathogenesis, and platforms for drug screening (Di Lullo and Kriegstein, 2017). They already offer much more than existing animal-models, and the development of this tool just only recently began.

However, while cerebral organoids indeed seem to hold a lot of promise to become the next most common and most adequate model for studying human neurodevelopment, there are multiple challenges that have to be addressed in the future. How widely this technique will be used and adopted depends on how scientists will tackle existing technical challenges and improve upon the current protocol. Andrews and Nowakowski (2019) point out that there is a need for a larger pool of data-driven approaches for unbiased comparisons of brain organoids. Di Lullo and Kriegstein (2017) stress the importance of acknowledging both strengths and weaknesses of the existing protocol to improve upon it. They include the possibility of using cell lines derived directly from patients and relative ease of genomic manipulation among the number of advantages of cerebral organoids as *in vitro* system for experimentation purposes. However, the technique will clearly benefit from a systematic analysis of cell types generated that will also allow a robust and necessary comparison to *in vivo* counterparts. Lastly, Quadrato et al. (2016) argues that greater maturation and diversity of cell types will lead to a chance to analyze processes that were previously experimentally inaccessible (myelination and pruning of dendritic spines that are thought to underlie the tissue pathology seen in human patients).

There is nothing quite like the human brain, yet cerebral organoids, these unassuming clumps of reprogrammed stem cells, hold the remarkable potential to help scientists grasp what makes us human by allowing them to understand why our brain is so unique and how it develops in this particular way to surpass in complexity anything ever known to mankind.

# Works Cited

Andrews, Madeline G., and Tomasz J. Nowakowski. "'Human Brain Development through the Lens of Cerebral Organoid Models.'" *Brain Research*, Sept. 2019, p. 146470. *ScienceDirect*, doi:10.1016/j.brainres.2019.146470.

Di Lullo, Elizabeth, and Arnold R. Kriegstein. "The Use of Brain Organoids to Investigate Neural Development and Disease." *Nature Reviews Neuroscience*, vol. 18, no. 10, Oct. 2017, pp. 573–84. *www-nature-com.proxy.lib.umich.edu*, doi:10.1038/nrn.2017.107.

Kelava, Iva, and Madeline A. Lancaster. "Stem Cell Models of Human Brain Development." *Cell Stem Cell*, vol. 18, no. 6, June 2016, pp. 736–48. *ScienceDirect*, doi:10.1016/j.stem.2016.05.022.

Lancaster, Madeline A., et al. "Cerebral Organoids Model Human Brain Development and Microcephaly." *Nature*, vol. 501, no. 7467, Sept. 2013, pp. 373–79. *www-nature-com.proxy.lib.umich.edu*, doi:10.1038/nature12517.

Lou, Yan-Ru Lou, and Leung, Alan W. "Next Generation Organoids For Biomedical Research and Applications.", *Biotechnology Advances*, vol. 36, no. 1, 2018, pp. 132-149. https://doi.org/10.1016/j.biotechadv.2017.10.005.

Luo, Chongyuan, et al. "Cerebral Organoids Recapitulate Epigenomic Signatures of the Human Fetal Brain." *Cell Reports*, vol. 17, no. 12, Dec. 2016, pp. 3369–84. *ScienceDirect*, doi:10.1016/j.celrep.2016.12.001.

Marshall, Jonothon J., and John O. Mason. "Mouse vs Man: Organoid Models of Brain Development & Disease." *Brain Research*, vol. 1724, Dec. 2019, p. 146427. *ScienceDirect*, doi:10.1016/j.brainres.2019.146427.

Pollen, Alex A., et al. "Establishing Cerebral Organoids as Models of Human-Specific Brain Evolution." *Cell*, vol. 176, no. 4, Feb. 2019, pp. 743-756. e17. *ScienceDirect*, doi:10.1016/j.cell.2019.01.017.

Quadrato, Giorgia, et al. "The Promises and Challenges of Human Brain Organoids as Models of Neuropsychiatric Disease." *Nature Medicine*, vol. 22, no. 11, Nov. 2016, pp. 1220–28. *www-nature-com.proxy.lib.umich.edu*, doi:10.1038/nm.4214.

Rakic, Pasko. "Elusive Radial Glial Cells: Historical and Evolutionary Perspective." *Glia*, vol. 43 (2003), pp. 19-32, Wiley Online Library. https://onlinelibrary-wiley-com.proxy.lib.umich.edu/doi/full/10.1002/glia.10244.

Sasai, Yoshiki. "Next-Generation Regenerative Medicine: Organogenesis from Stem Cells in 3D Culture." *Cell Stem Cell*, vol. 12, no. 5, May 2013, pp. 520–30. *ScienceDirect*, doi:10.1016/j.stem.2013.04.009.

Temple, Sally. "Division and Differentiation of Isolated CNS Blast Cells in Microculture." *Nature*, vol. 340, no. 6233, Aug. 1989, pp. 471–73. *www-nature-com.proxy.lib.umich.edu*, doi:10.1038/340471a0.

Trujillo, Cleber A., et al. "Complex Oscillatory Waves Emerging from Cortical Organoids Model Early Human Brain Network Development." *Cell Stem Cell*, Aug. 2019. *ScienceDirect*, doi:10.1016/j.stem.2019.08.002.

# Excellence in Upper-Level Writing (Sciences)

## Gene editing for the 21st century: CRISPR/Cas9 and Prime Editing
by Franco Tavella

*From BIOPHYS 450/550: Intro to Biophys Lab*
*Nominated by Qiong Yang*

This hands-on laboratory course, Biophysics 450/550 Techniques in Biophysics, not only trains students in the design of experiments, data collection and analysis, but also requires a substantial amount of writing in a scientific fashion. At the end of each laboratory session of six individual experimental modules, each student has to describe the scientific problem that the experiment addressed, the experimental approach used, the results of their measurements and the interpretation of the data in the context of the original problem. Additionally, each must explore and present a topic of their own interest in greater depth in a final report. Throughout the semester, Franco has constantly demonstrated the highest-level scientific writing skill for all six laboratory reports. His reports have been unanimously rated the best by our graduate student instructor (GSI), undergraduate teaching assistant, and myself as the instructor of this course. In this final report, Franco has showcased his excellent scientific writing by comprehensively reviewing CRISPR technology, a revolutionary breakthrough for genetics and evolution. Ever since the hallmark discovery of CRISPR/Cas9, an innate adaptive immune system bacterium uses to defend themselves against phages, it has attracted enormous interest in scientists and societies. This simple yet powerful cutting and pasting mechanism originally from old prokaryotes can be repurposed to alter DNA sequences and modify gene function in almost any complex organism including humans, and thus promises a wide variety of applications from correcting genetic defects to treating and preventing diseases. Franco has first given a comprehensive literature review of the history, background, development, and fundamental mechanism of the classic CRISPR/Cas9, the most popular and well-known CRISPR technology so far. Intriguingly, he has also discussed the limitations of the current CRISPR and has further elucidated one of the most promising recent advances of this everchanging technology, Prime Editing. He compared the classic CRISPR/Cas9 and the newly published Prime Editing to demonstrate how Prime Editing can efficiently improve specificity, one of the major challenges in CRISPR/Cas9.

-- *Qiong Yang*

# Gene editing for the 21st century: CRISPR/Cas9 and Prime Editing

Manipulating genetic information in biological systems is an essential tool for research and clinical applications. Nowadays, user-defined plasmids can be easily transfected into bacteria to obtain fully functional proteins using well-established protocols. However, manipulating eukaryotic systems with such precision has remained an elusive challenge. Over the last decades, scientists have been developing new tools to micro-edit nucleic acids in eukaryotic cells. The most prominent one is a technique that harnesses the prokaryotic immune response: the CRISPR/Cas9 system. In this report, we will review the main features of CRISPR/Cas9 and its gene-editing capabilities. Additionally, we will describe a recently developed technique: Prime Editing which addresses many disadvantages present in CRISPR/Cas9. Interestingly, Prime editing introduces a novel feature to the realm of gene editing: the target and the edition are encoded in the same molecule. The field of gene editing seems to be flourishing to address the challenges of the current century.

## CRISPR/Cas9 is a sequence-specific DNA-cutting tool

In many bacteria and archaea, a DNA sequence called CRISPR serves as a memory of past bacteriophage attacks [1]. The structure of this sequence is very particular: previous infections are encoded between non-contiguous spacers. Also, a family of proteins called Cas can destroy invading agents with their nuclease function. This adaptive immune system works by combining the CRISPR gene with Cas nucleases. The gene is transcribed and matured to generate the CRISPR RNA (crRNA). This RNA binds to Cas nucleases and guides them to the specific DNA sequences of known infections. Finally, Cas/crRNA cleaves DNA in both strands and inactivates the invading agent.

Three different types of CRISPR-Cas systems have been extensively studied [1]. They differ in the crRNA production mechanism and the Cas proteins involved. The most studied systems, known as Type II, have received increasing attention because they have a minimal set of components: two RNA molecules and a single Cas protein known as Cas9. In these systems, a trans-activating CRISPR RNA (tracrRNA) guides the maturation of crRNA and its anchoring to Cas9. Ultimately, crRNA, tracrRNA, and Cas9 form the active ribonucleoprotein complex of the immune response [2]. Two factors determine successful DNA cleavage. First, crRNA and DNA have to share a 20 nucleotide complementary sequence [3]. Second, a 3 nucleotide sequence, known as Proto-spacer Adjacent Motif (PAM), needs to be present in the target DNA [4].

## Combining CRISPR/Cas9 with DNA repair systems provides a powerful gene-editing platform

In an award-winning article, Jinek et al. [5] engineered CRISPR/Cas9 to make programmable DNA cuts. They created a simplified genomic tool by linking the crRNA and tracrRNA together. The new system is composed of only two biomolecules: a single guide RNA (gRNA) and the Cas9 protein (see Figure 1A). After this milestone, Cong et al. [6] showed that the same tool can produce user-defined editions. Multiple genetic editions were achieved in mammalian systems by combining DNA repair pathways with a Cas9 nickase. A nickase is a protein that only cuts one DNA strand. Two different protein domains of Cas 9 cleave each strand: HNH and Ruv-C. Interestingly, Cas9 can be converted into a nickase by the inactivation of any of these domains.

Currently, the gene edition pipeline consists of Cas9 DNA-cutting followed by DNA repair. Two techniques are commonly used for the last step: Non-Homologous End Joining (NHEJ) and Homology-Directed Repair (HDR) [7]. In NHEJ, DNA is stitched together with random insertions or deletions (indels) [8]. This feature makes the method suitable for gene silencing. In HDR, an extra DNA molecule containing the desired edition is added [9]. This molecule guides the repairing and establishes the modification. Preferentially, HDR is used to insert or delete large DNA portions.

**CRISPR/Cas9 is efficient for gene silencing but limited for insertions**

Multiple factors contribute to the precision and accuracy of gene edition by the CRISPR/Cas9 system. On the one hand, different target sequences have different Cas9 affinities [10]. One contributing element to this is the ratio of purine to pyrimidine in the gRNA. Several models have been developed for predicting a target's efficiency and facilitate experimental design [11]. On the other hand, Cas9 produces DNA breaks in untargeted locations [12]. Different methods are being developed to detect, characterize and minimize this effect [13]. However, the interplay between DNA excision and repair is the main factor affecting the edition outcome.

The efficiency of gene edition is greatly affected by the characteristics of the DNA repair systems [14]. The NHEJ pathway, although error-prone, is convenient for gene knockouts. Its repair proteins are present throughout the cell cycle and achieve edition efficiencies of 20-60%. On the other hand, for precise insertions or deletions, the HDR pathway is preferable. However, it is only present in phases S and G2 of the cell cycle and has an inherent low activity. Combined with the competition between HDR and NHEJ for DNA repair, the efficiency ranges from 0.5 to 20%. Recent research addressed this issue by inhibiting a key protein of the NHEJ pathway [15]. The modification improved HDR gene editing up to 19-fold. In conclusion, precise insertions using CRISPR/Cas9 are still challenging.

**Prime editing: a search-and-replace genomic tool**

Improving the state of the art of gene editing, Anzalone et al. [16] developed Prime Editing: a technique that doesn't require double-strand DNA breaks nor donor DNA templates. Researchers developed a chimeric protein-RNA complex termed Prime Editor (PE). The protein in the complex is a Cas9 nickase fused to a reverse-transcriptase (RT). Besides, the engineered RNA contains the genetic locus of interest and the edit to install. Using the name of the newly created technique, this component was termed prime editing guide RNA (pegRNA). See Figure 1B for a sketch of the system.

Prime editing targets the DNA and installs the desired edit in situ. First, the nickase, guided by the RNA, liberates one strand of the target loci. Then, the fused RT extends the created flap with the desired edit encoded in pegRNA. Afterward, the endogenous nucleases FEN1 and EXO1 cleave the unedited flap of the DNA. Finally, the DNA repair system establishes the edit. In comparison to editing with CRISPR/Cas9 mediated by HDR, no donor DNA nor double-strand DNA break is needed. In terms of efficiency, the method is similar to CRISPR/Cas9-HDR but with greatly reduced indel production and off-target editions.

**Gene editing for the 21st century**

A sketch of the systems discussed in this report is presented in Figure 1. Additionally, an illustrative result taken from [16] is shown for a direct comparison between the CRISPR/Cas9 and Prime editing. The indels produced by CRISPR/Cas9 exceed those of Prime editing by nearly 70%. Nevertheless, the percentage of correct edits by both methods is comparable with some results more favorable for Prime editing.

Gene editing can cure diseases [16] or push forward the field of mammalian synthetic biology [17]. Without doubt these techniques will revolutionize medicine and academic research in the 21st century. Therefore, we need to have the necessary discussions [18] before that time comes.

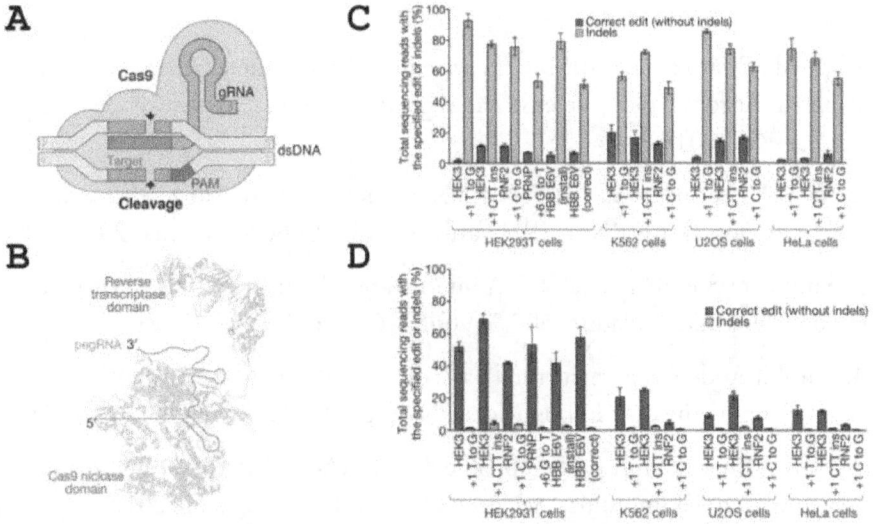

Figure 1: CRISPR/Cas9 and Prime editing. The engineered version of CRISPR/ Cas9 (Panel A) is composed of the nuclease Cas9 and a guide RNA (gRNA) which contains a target sequence of 20 nucleotides [5]. The macromolecular complex recognizes the DNA target downstream a PAM sequence and cleaves both strands. Prime editing protein (Panel B) is a chimera comprised of a reverse-transcriptase and a Cas9 nickase [16]. The target sequence and the desired edition are encoded in a single RNA molecule termed prime editing guiding RNA (pegRNA). Different genetic editions were tested in Cas9-HDR and Prime editing for comparison (Panel C and D respectively). The indels produced by CRISPR/Cas9 exceed those of Prime editing by nearly 70%. Nevertheless, the percentage of correct edits by both methods is comparable with some results more favorable for Prime editing. Panel A was designed by Marius Walter. Panels B, C, and D are taken from [16].

# References

1. Devaki Bhaya et al. CRISPR-cas systems in bacteria and archaea: versatile small RNAs for adaptive defense and regulation. Annual Review of Genetics, 45:273–297, 2011.

2. Elitza Deltcheva et al. CRISPR RNA maturation by trans-encoded small RNA and host factor RNase III. Nature, 471(7340):602–607, mar 2011.

3. Samuel H Sternberg et al. DNA interrogation by the CRISPR RNA-guided endonuclease Cas9. Nature, 507(7490):62–67, mar 2014.

4. Carolin Anders et al. Structural basis of PAM-dependent target DNA recognition by the cas9 Endonuclease. Nature, 513(7519):569–573, sep 2014.

5. Martin Jinek et al. A programmable dual-RNA-guided DNA endonuclease in adaptive bacterial immunity. Science, 337(6096):816–821, aug 2012.

6. Le Cong et al. Multiplex genome engineering using CRISPR/cas systems. Science, 339(6121):819–823, feb 2013.

7. Claire Wyman et al. DNA double-strand break repair: all's well that ends well. Annual. Review of Genetics, 40:363–383, 2006.

8. Mireille Bétermier et al. Is non-homologous end-joining really an inherently error-prone process?. PLoS Genetics, 10(1):e1004086, jan 2014.

9. G A Cromie et al. Recombination at double-strand breaks and DNA ends: conserved mechanisms from phage to humans. Molecular Cell, 8(6):1163–1174, dec 2001.

10. Han Xu et al. Sequence determinants of improved CRISPR sgRNA design. Genome Research, 25(8):1147–1157, aug 2015.

11. Shengdar Q Tsai et al. GUIDE-seq enables genome-wide profiling of off-target cleavage by CRISPR-cas nucleases. Nature Biotechnology, 33(2):187–197, feb 2015.

12. Jinzhi Duan et al. Genome-wide identification of CRISPR/cas9 off-targets in human Genome. Cell Research, 24(8):1009–1012, aug 2014.

13. Benjamin P Kleinstiver et al. High-fidelity CRISPR-cas9 nucleases with no detectable genome-wide off-target effects. Nature, 529(7587):490–495, jan 2016.

14. Hui Yang et al. One-step generation of mice carrying reporter and conditional alleles by CRISPR/cas-mediated genome engineering. Cell, 154(6):1370–1379, sep 2013.

15. Takeshi Maruyama et al. Increasing the efficiency of precise genome editing with CRISPR-cas9 by inhibition of nonhomologous end joining. Nature Biotechnology, 33 (5):538–542, may 2015.

16. Andrew V Anzalone et al. Search-and-replace genome editing without double-strand breaks or donor DNA. Nature, 576(7785):149–157, oct 2019.

17. Tackhoon Kim et al. CRISPR/cas-based devices for mammalian synthetic biology. Current Opinion in Chemical Biology, 52:23–30, oct 2019.

18. Adam P Cribbs et al. Science and bioethics of CRISPR-cas9 gene editing: An analysis towards separating facts and fiction. The Yale journal of biology and medicine, 90(4):625–634, dec 2017.

# Excellence in Upper-Level Writing (Social Sciences)

## D.C. Dog Fight: Principle and Pragmatism of the Bush-era Supreme Court
by Max Steinbaum
*From POLSCI 319: Politics of Civil Liberties and Civil Rights*
*Nominated by Jacob Walden*

Max Steinbaum took a constrained assignment: a short word count, a laundry list of objectives to achieve in discussing Supreme Court power, and a large corpus of case law -- and crafted a thoughtful, engaging piece with nuanced analysis of the American judiciary. It is rare for students tasked with these essays to produce a compelling set of claims for evaluation, and only a few provide original, nuanced analysis. Max achieves this while also weaving in a literary flair and set of animal-based imagery. Max is addressing not only the Court as a static institution, but how it dynamically alters the scope of its rulings to maximize a balance of two forms of Court power. He provides sophisticated analysis is delineating how the Court may change its logic of response, and why its strategic decision-making may shift as circumstances and actors change. This is advanced, theory-building analysis, and manages to address the seemingly contradictory evidence given to students about Supreme Court rulings. We delighted in reading Max's work. It is easily the best product in the last few years of this course, out of over 1,000 essays written.

*-- Jacob Walden*

# D.C. Dog Fight: Principle and Pragmatism of the Bush-era Supreme Court

According to 19th-century humorist Mark Twain, "It's not the size of the dog in the fight -- it's the size of the fight in the dog" (Graham, 2015). The author of *Huckleberry Finn* evidently did not understand the practical dynamics of fang-to-fang scuffles, because most physical confrontations between a chihuahua and a doberman, regardless of the former's determination, will inevitably end poorly for the smaller canine. As numerous Supreme Court cases regarding Guantanamo demonstrate, SCOTUS -- a rather insistent chihuahua -- routinely asserted the rights of detainees against a united executive/ legislative front pursuing rights-denial for expediency. Despite the Court's theoretical coequality *and* numerous legal victories of Guantanamo defendants, the prescriptions of Supreme Court rulings concerning detention were repeatedly circumvented by a Bush administration determined to prosecute the War on Terror on its own terms. Finding itself cornered by hostile neoconservative dobermans and appreciating these *de facto* power dynamics, the Supreme Court deliberately narrowed the scope of its decisions in the hope of enhancing the efficacy of its rulings. Through this conscientious narrowing, SCOTUS maintained its resolve to curb Bush's overextensions in a refusal to kowtow to the forces of practical power, as it had done historically in times of war. As such, the trajectory of Guantanamo-era jurisprudence conveys two realities of Court power: 1) that a great disparity exists between the *theoretical* and *practical* (that is, realistic ability to stop executive/ legislative constitutional overreaches) power of the Court, as the latter requires the cooperation of the other branches, but 2) the Court can actually *increase* its practical power by narrowing its prescriptive focus and accepting smaller victories.

While the Supreme Court's rulings repeatedly affirmed the rights of Guantanamo detainees, practical powers possessed by the executive allowed the Bush administration to circumvent judicial direction, which it did repeatedly. The first such executive maneuver occurred following *Hamdi v. Rumsfeld* and

*Rasul v. Bush*, in which the Supreme Court held that the Due Process Clause guarantees Americans designated as "enemy combatants" by the executive branch the ability to challenge their status and detention (*Hamdi*), and that non-citizen Guantanamo prisoners were entitled to petition for *habeas corpus* (*Rasul*) -- sweeping claims that affirmed the rights of U.S. and foreign detainees alike, and in a broader sense, marked the first major judicial attempt to restrict the president's power to unilaterally prosecute the War on Terror. Since the War's 2001 inauguration, the Bush administration had done so through John Yoo's "unitary executive" justification, a doctrine stipulating that the president, as commander-in-chief, has virtually plenary power over military and intelligence-collecting affairs (Brandwein lecture, 11/12/19.) Determined to preserve this arrangement to the best of its ability, Congress -- allied with the president -- overwhelmingly passed the Detainee Treatment Act of 2005, which directed the establishment of CSRTs for Guantanamo detainees to challenge their "enemy combatant" designations. The kangaroo-esque nature of the CSRTs, however, effectively allowed the Bush administration to circumvent the Court's prescriptions and oversee detention as it desired (Brandwein lecture, 11/12/19). Two years later, the Supreme Court pushed back: Further asserting detainee rights in *Hamdan v. Rumsfeld*, the Court ruled that the terribly flawed military commissions did not sufficiently respect plaintiff rights as guaranteed by the UCMJ and Geneva Conventions; the AUMF, SCOTUS pronounced, does *not* allow the president to violate these codes, and more specific legislation would be necessary to assert such executive authority. In direct response, Congress passed the Military Commissions Act of 2006, which, in authorizing the military tribunals in question, legislatively enshrined the executive power challenged by the Supreme Court. A pattern here is plainly discernable: despite the Court's constitutional justness, routine Congressional/ executive maneuvering -- made possible through their pooled practical power -- substantially defanged Supreme Court pronouncements that ran counter to their preferences.

Tacitly recognizing its practical limitations but still hoping to constrain the Bush administration's successful circumventions, the Supreme Court deliberately narrowed the scope of its decisions in the hope of enhancing the efficacy of its rulings -- a strategy that in some ways *expanded* Court power. As discussed, the Court cast a wide prescriptive net in *Hamdi* and *Rasul*; were it fully respected by Congress and the president, it would have materially blunted the power over detention so far enjoyed by the executive branch. The establishment of CSRTs overtly communicated that the Bush administration would circumvent inconvenient jurisprudence. As the next major Guantanamo decision (*Hamdan v. Rumsfeld*) demonstrates, the Supreme Court recognized this reality and inaugurated a strategy of "scope narrowing" to ensure the observation of its rulings, to certain success. In *Hamdan*, SCOTUS targeted Guantanamo military commissions procedure, and the need for Congressional authorization for these tribunals to continue -- a ruling with far more *specific* ramifications, but still allowing the Court to check executive oversteps. Congress's passage of the MCA of 2006 contained concessions to this effect, as the Act affirmed certain detainee rights (e.g. knowledge of charges), and respected the *Hamdan* stipulation that the military tribunals required legislative authorization (Brandwein lecture, 11/14/19). In this way, the response to *Hamdan* departed from the wholesale circumvention witnessed after *Hamdi* and *Rasul*. This is not to suggest, however, that "narrowing" was universally effective; rather, its success was mixed. As Scheppele correctly observes, SCOTUS decisions that "stood up to the government and laid down limits on anti-terror policy" had little *practical* effect, as executive/ Congressional sidesteps allowed the Bush administration to continue "treat[ing] suspected terrorists" as it desired -- reflecting, as Lemieux and Lovell observe, that "elected officials have numerous available weapons for limiting the impact of judicial rulings" (11). As such, the Court's narrowing did not yield meteoric change -- but neither was this the Court's objective. In accepting the reality of executive maneuvering (as occurred after *Hamdi* and *Rasul*), the Court's scope limitation represented a deliberate pursuit of *smaller* victories to maintain a degree of practical influence.

Strategic prescriptive narrowing -- evidence of the Court's resolve to curb executive excess -- demonstrated principled insistence on the part of the judicial branch, in a departure from its historical deference to practical power in times of war. In *Korematsu*, for instance, the Supreme Court found itself in a precarious predicament: it could condemn Japanese internment, and in doing so render a decision that may have been ignored by the other branches, or uphold existing policy in pursuit of non-confrontational deference. In a jurisprudential kowtow, SCOTUS selected the latter, safer route that ensured the preservation of its legitimacy. Six decades on, the Supreme Court again found itself pitted against a united executive/ legislative front in a time of war. Rather than heel as in *Korematsu*, SCOTUS's decisions regarding Guantanamo detainees -- even though increasingly limited in scope -- were guided by a common principle of reigning in constitutional transgressions by the other branches. As best seen in *Boumediene v. Bush*, the Supreme Court majority considered its promotion of detainee rights to be a principled stand asserting constitutional checks (and therein its own authority), and that it even operated with the sanction of the Founders. Drawing a line in the sand, the majority opinion forcefully pronounced that even in times of war, "the Nation's basic charter cannot be contracted away [....] To hold that the political branches may switch the Constitution on or off at will would lead to a regime in which they, not this Court, say 'what the law is'" (*Boumediene v. Bush*, 2008).

Part of the Supreme Court's practical ineffectuality is structural: as a reacting branch with no enforcement mechanism, the Court can only address constitutional violations *ex post facto*, and even then only really offer commentary. As such, even as Guantanamo defendants achieved a series of paper victories, "little changed in the situation that they went to court to challenge" on account of practical power residing outside the Supreme Court (Scheppele, 2012). As the trajectory of Guantanamo cases relate, SCOTUS learned early on that a chihuahua is unwise to charge at a doberman. In sharpening its prescriptive focus, however, the Supreme Court was able to score measured victories -- and in doing so, it sounded an unprecedented growl against executive/ legislative wartime breaches.

# Excellence in Upper-Level Writing (Social Sciences)

## The Plastic Problem: What are Scientists doing to Reduce their Environmental Footprint?
by Maryellen Zbrozek

*From ENVIRON 320: Environmental Journalism*
*Nominated by Julie Halpert*

For the class I co-teach, Environ 320, Maryellen chose to write a news feature entitled: "The Plastic Problem: What are Scientists Doing to Reduce their Environmental Footprint?" She identified an intriguing and important topic: the role that scientists play in generating plastics waste, ironically in pursuit of their discoveries to help the environment. But she didn't just discuss the state of the problem. She advanced the story to reveal interesting solutions that a variety of scientists are pioneering. Maryellen found leading experts both at the University of Michigan and in other parts of the country to interview and included compelling quotes from them. The article is perfectly organized and is easy to follow, communicated in an extremely effective way. It's not bogged down with scientific jargon and is written in a manner that the average person can easily understand. I was particularly impressed by the high caliber of writing. She has a captivating an emotional beginning, with a story of a scientist who illustrates the issue she plans to explore. She provides an in-depth investigation of the issue, yet manages to keep the reader engaged. The article never seems redundant or mired in unnecessary details. The piece ends with a powerful, forward-looking quote that nicely sums up the situation Maryellen's article contains all the elements of an exemplary piece of writing. The piece is comparable to the quality of articles written by professional journalists.

*-- Julie Halpert*

# The Plastic Problem: What are Scientists doing to Reduce their Environmental Footprint?

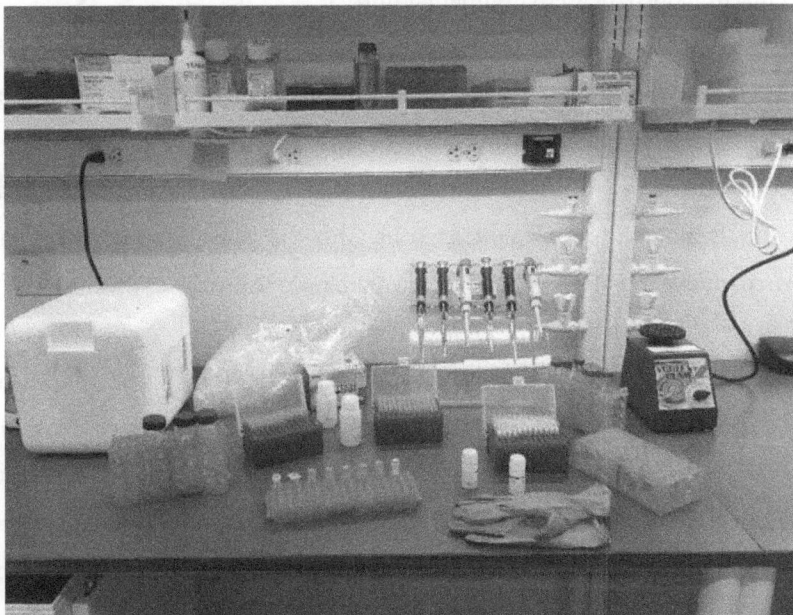

Like this microbiology lab at the University of Michigan, many scientific labs use high volumes of single-use plastics to conduct their research.

Rachel Cable uses as little plastic as possible in her daily life. She's an avid recycler, uses as many reusable products as possible, and avoids using single-use plastics. But when Cable, a scientist in the Environmental Viral Ecology Lab at the University of Michigan, heads to work, she's surrounded by the plastic she so pointedly avoids in the rest of her life. Cable, who studies microorganisms living on microplastics in oceans and lakes, not only uses plastic as a subject of study, but also uses plastic laboratory equipment to conduct her experiments. "Just by paying attention, you start to see plastic everywhere when you start doing this type of research," says Cable, who views scientific lab waste to be a huge problem.

A 2015 estimate from scientists at the University of Exeter indicated that scientific labs produce approximately 5.5 million tons of plastic waste annually. Considering that approximately eight million tons of plastic waste enters the world's oceans each year, according to the United Nations Environment Programme, the amount of plastic waste produced by science has prompted scientific institutions to implement programs, such as the University of Michigan's Sustainable Labs Program, to reduce their environmental impact.

"After doing this project [on microplastics], we try to be really conscientious of plastic waste. But we're also a microbiology lab. To be sterile is to be disposable, which is kind of disgusting," says Cable. In some cases, single-use plastic items are viewed as a necessity in the lab to maintain sterility or to prevent contaminating recycling streams with hazardous chemicals. Although research could be conducted using reusable materials like glass, Cable says that there just is not the infrastructure available to clean reusable items, nor is there the time.

"It's a problem where it's being used excessively, where they're using more than they need to use," says Anika Ballent, Education Director at Algalita, a California-based marine research and education center focusing on plastic pollution. Ballent believes that in some cases, plastic is the best alternative or the only option for certain chemicals or sample analyses. "Our issue with this material is not that it exists. It's not inherently bad. It's just that we are using it very irresponsibly," says Ballent. "That is what we need to change, not that we stop using it altogether."

At the University of Michigan, many scientists are part of the movement to be more environmentally conscious in the lab. Over 200 labs are taking part in the university's Sustainable Labs Program, an initiative started in 2014 by Dr. Sudhakar Reddy with the Office of Campus Sustainability. Alongside its efforts to reduce energy use and to minimize the use of hazardous chemicals, the Sustainable Labs Program also provides labs with many opportunities to recycle materials that would otherwise be thrown into the landfill.

"What's being done is about the biggest effort currently possible, and that's just from a lab safety point of view," says Ken Keeler, Senior Sustainability Rep in charge of the Sustainable Labs Program. To prevent people and the environment from being exposed to hazardous lab waste, any waste that has contacted hazardous material must be thrown in the landfill or incinerated. Other waste products, such as plastic boxes, cardboard, plastic bottles used for non-hazardous liquids, and some disposable gloves, are easily recycled by labs that participate in the Sustainable Labs Program.

To successfully recycle these types of materials, people at the university are working with manufacturers to get these materials recycled. The University of Michigan's biggest recycling program is their pipette tip box program. Pipettes, which are instruments used to transfer small amounts of liquid, require plastic tips that must be discarded once in contact with biologic samples or chemicals. These tips are stored in plastic boxes that prevent the tips from being contaminated. According to Keeler, recycling organizations at the university recognized pipette tip boxes as a huge source of plastic waste, so they contacted the manufacturer, Fisher Scientific, about it. As a result, Fisher sponsors the university's pipette tip box recycling program. According to Keeler, this program prevents 10-15 tons of plastic waste from ending up in Michigan landfills each year.

Despite their efforts to reduce plastic waste, manufacturers pose the largest challenge to lab waste reduction efforts, according to Keeler. He states that the most significant way to reduce waste is by minimizing it during production. "You can really reduce your waste by talking to the vendors and just getting them to not put as much packing material in," says Keeler.

Some manufacturers are responding to these concerns. Labcon, a company in Petaluma, California, markets themselves as the first lab supply company to sell products with sustainability in mind. Although organizations like the University of Michigan's Office of Campus Sustainability view plastic waste as a necessity based on the need for sterile equipment, Labcon tries to make this equipment as minimally wasteful as possible.

According to Scott Weitze, Lead Scientist at Labcon, the company focuses on how to determine which parts of a scientific instrument must be single-use and which parts are not necessary for the function of the device. To accomplish this, the company designs products to be reusable and refillable with minimal packaging. When possible, Labcon uses fully-recyclable materials and bioplastics.

"In terms of who is in the biotech industry, it's often people who care more about the environment and tend to be pretty educated on topics like global climate change. It's a strange fit in that the people who care most about these issues, they're in an industry that uses a *ton* of plastic," says Weitze. But the scientists are not usually the agents in charge of purchasing lab materials. Weitze says that the way to be sustainable under the current lab infrastructure is to flip the cost of sustainable products like those produced by Labcon, or to alter the mindset of lab purchasing agents to encourage them to be more sustainability-minded. Cable and Keeler agree.

In the meantime, Ballent believes that the future looks positive for reducing scientific plastic waste. Chemical recycling, an up-and-coming technology, has the potential to change the way society uses plastics. Chemical recycling breaks plastics down differently than the melting and remolding that is standardly used on recycled plastics. Done at a higher temperature and pressure by companies like Loop Industries, this technology disassembles plastic products into individual molecules, which allows for the separation of hazardous materials from those that can be safely recycled into new plastics or converted into fuel.

"There's a lot of unknowns about it, so we'll have to wait and see," Ballent says about chemical recycling. Despite these unknowns, she is confident that this technology could be used on plastic waste from scientific labs.

Until technologies like chemical recycling become more mainstream, environmentalists such as Michael Murray, a staff scientist at the National Wildlife Federation, are encouraged by the efforts research institutions are making to reduce their environmental footprint. "You need some type of program like the one at Michigan to try to really address this issue and improve recycling rates or reduce the amount of waste generation," says Murray. He encourages sustainable lab programs to expand further, into being educational tools. "In teaching labs, we can encourage students to be thinking about these issues more. Regardless of what work they're going to be doing afterwards, if they're aware that there are ways to reuse or reduce the use of plastics for a particular application, then they can take those lessons learned into other work they wind up doing later on."

# Excellence in Upper-Level Writing (Humanities)

## عنوان

by Jinan Abufarha

*From WRITING 300: Seminar in Peer Writing Consultation*
*Nominated by Christine Modey*

Jinan's first essay for our peer writing consultant training course represents the best kind of re-vision in which a writer stretches beyond their own first imaginings and the constraints of the assignment to uncover new layers in their own experiences and the broader universe of ideas. Jinan's autoethnography has a strong voice and also a strong, complex focus on exploring the tension and oppression she's experienced throughout her education and how she grappled with that as a person, a student, and a writer. Jinan uses Paulo Friere's ideas of liberatory pedagogy to put her experience into a broader framework that allows her to critique typical educational practices. This essay is a poignant exploration of Jinan's double consciousness and the tension between mastering the the dominant discourse of Standard English and valuing her home discourse and Arab identity.

-- *Christine Modey*

# عنوان

My first memory is candlelight. My *sito* holding my tiny hand in her own-- wrinkled and scarred, a memento of a life she is no longer sure she lived-- and reading the lines on my palms. She loved to tell me stories in Arabic. I would sit on her lap, in a city lost to hindsight, and hang onto words I didn't have to understand to know were beautiful.

I am a compilation of stories. I am the apple seeds Eve spat out. I am the footsteps of the *Bedouin* in the sand. I am those who wait and those who died waiting. I am a careless cultural transplant job. My bones still echo my grandfather's laugh and my heart beats to the drum he played to drown the noise of people rioting outside. I am held together by empty pleasures: *Gossip Girl* references, Vines and the quiet moments I am neither here nor there.

Being displaced would always be my parent's greatest heartbreak but through us they had an opportunity to preserve their culture in a foreign world. Learning Arabic was neither optional nor recommended but framed as essential to our survival. This all or nothing mentality produced a sense of anxiety in me. As a child, I didn't understand the significance of language and thought, or the idea of language as a gateway to culture. I did understand the disappointed furrow of my father's brow when I mispronounced a word in Arabic or the embarrassment on my mother's face when my grandfather made fun of my American accent.

My life can only be equated to a Turkish soap opera: poorly translated and almost artistically melodramatic. It is always in this unreachable dialect, somewhere between Arabic and English. I started writing to figure out what gets lost in translation, to create a space for this inner world I could never vocalize. Writing has been and always will be an act of becoming for me. The way I write and learned to write is an extension of how I view myself in the world.

The first classroom I ever inhabited was an Islamic private school. For the first 7 years of my life, I existed within a bubble that insulated me from mainstream, American society. I didn't know that I was "non-traditional"; I was not a minority at school. I was surrounded by people who looked like me. That might be cliché to say but is a comfort taken for granted when you are in the majority. There is a safety in being able to "see" yourself. I learned Arabic at this school just as you would English in any other. I spoke in Arabic, read poetry in Arabic, wrote short stories in Arabic. Eventually, the costs of private school outweighed the perceived benefits of being surrounded by entirely Arabs and my parents transferred me into an American public school in a predominantly white city.

Here, I'll clarify that I spoke perfect English (for a third grader). On weekends, I would totter out of the library with a stack of books bigger than me. This was always to the frustration of my mother who insisted I would never finish them before the due date. However, books were my window to American society, and I gladly jumped through that window. Despite being born and raised in America, the culture was exotic to me. The freedom, individuality, it was all foreign. I grew up in a culture that valued community, obligations. I found the things that American characters were preoccupied with fascinating. I held such an idealized image of American schools in my head and, guiltily, I envied that lifestyle.

The transition between schools fully popped that idealized bubble. When I transferred, the administration took one look at my file, saw I had gone to school in Dearborn and put me in ESL without even testing me to make sure I needed it. Every day, I was marched out of class along with the rest of the minorities. None of us understood *why*, but we were clearly being marked. I knew I didn't need to be pulled out of class or need remedial English. I came home every day sobbing to my mother about my second English class and a test I was always one or two points off from passing. The school district didn't care how I felt or about acclimating me to a totally new environment; they just wanted to cash a funding check.

In *Pedagogy of the Oppressed*, Paulo Freire explores the way that our relationships with society are not only reproduced but formulated in the classroom. He says, "The oppressed are regarded as the pathology of healthy society, which must therefore adjust these 'incompetent and lazy'. . . need to be 'integrated,' 'incorporated', into the healthy society that they have 'forsaken'" (Friere 74). A lot of the kids in my ESL class were first generation and born in America. We had English proficiency on par with our peers. Yet, we acted a little different, came from non-white cities and ate our "bizarre" lunches. The public show of removing the ethnic minorities from the classroom was a shaming act. It sent the message to both us and our classmates that there was something wrong with us that needed to be corrected. *Something* about us had to be "fixed" so that we could be assimilated into productive, American society. So that we could deserve to learn in the same space as our white peers.

This was setting us up for how we lived in the real world. By separating most of the minorities from the rest of class and creating that distinction the school became a microcosm of America. They were writing race consciousness into us. When we went out into the real world, we would be reproducing the sort of stereotypes and divides that were put into place in the classroom. I don't ever remember sitting with the white kids at lunch or playing with anyone other than the Arabs or Chaldeans during recess. We segregated ourselves in the same way the adults did because at that point in our lives we saw them as all-knowing. Our learning process consisted of absorbing the lessons they gave to us.

The most psychologically damaging part of being in ESL was the subliminal framework surrounding it. As Paulo Freire said, we were "'welfare recipients'" (Friere 74). We were supposed to look at these extra classes as a gift bestowed on us. The school system didn't *have* to give us extra classes, but they *wanted* to *help* us. They were doing us a favor. We had absolute ignorance projected onto us so that we would internalize the fact that we were inferior. They had to Other us, make us conscious of our position on the fringes of civil society, so we would blindly embrace whatever methods they claimed would make us successful. It was so crushing to me that I wasn't being embraced by this culture that I put on a pedestal for much of my younger life. I constantly wondered what made the white kids not want to interact with me. I started blaming the Arab food that my mom packed me for lunch, the way my name didn't quite fit in their mouths, even the curl of my hair. I became grateful when they didn't let us speak our native languages in class. I became more than willing to give up my home discourse and do anything to blend in.

I only took ESL classes for elementary school, but most of my experiences within school as an ethnic-minority mirrored this. I never had a subject position in my classroom. The world was something that happened to me rather than something I actively existed in. My educators were not interested in giving me the grammar to name my suffering nor to change the status of my oppression. Whether intentional or not, they molded my consciousness so that I adapted and embraced the structures of my oppression. I was robbed of that process of viewing, questioning and participating in my molding of reality. Rather, through our coursework, our curriculum, and content of our classes I was taught that reality was something to assimilate to. This was "just how the world was" and if I wanted to be successful then I had to be the thing that changed to fit the standard.

Learning, and learning to write, meant learning to camouflage myself. When I came home and my parents spoke to me in Arabic, I responded in English. I became obsessed with exclusively reading American "classics". I straightened my hair every single day for three years. I stayed out of the sun because I hated how dark I got. One day, I woke up and realized I had not even written my own name in Arabic in years.

My fear of existing outside the box was reaffirmed by the fact that the rare times I wrote in a non-standard way I was punished for it. Writing a poem about Palestine was enough to almost get me suspended in high school because a school board member took issue with me bringing "politics" into a creative space. I once wrote an essay about my experiences as a woman in a conservative Arab/Muslim household and the peers who reviewed it used the essay to condemn Arab culture as a whole. In 9th grade we had to write a research paper on a poet of our choice, and when I tried to write it about a very influential poet in the Arab world I was "encouraged" to try to find a more "recognizable" poet to write my essay about.

So, I just gave up. Obviously, my identity had no place in academic spaces. Somewhere along the line I got it into my head that my voice was not important, and no one wanted to hear *my* story. The model of education I was in valued acculturation and conformity and that reflected itself in my writing. I mainly wrote in a very standardized, academic mode of writing. I never wrote creatively, not in Arabic nor English. I certainly never wrote about my whole little life in the Middle East or the "Arab" parts of my childhood. I created compartments. My consciousness was fractured as I had to learn how to operate two entirely different cultures whether I was at home or in the world.

In hindsight, I recognize being able to code-switch (both linguistically and culturally) was a privilege. I had the option to switch between cultures and languages because (at least before I made the decision to white-wash myself and my writing) I was an equal participant in both cultural spheres. I had proficiency in both my home discourse and the dominant discourse. It was accessible to me, although at a cost. It wasn't empowering to master academic discourse. It didn't help translate my thoughts into language; it reshaped my thoughts.

It did, however, come with a certain level of success that I wouldn't have achieved if I totally rejected standard English or if I had prioritized my mother tongue over the one I'm currently writing in. If I hadn't wanted to be accepted by American society so badly, hadn't wanted all parts of myself to be translatable, I wouldn't enjoy many of the privileges I do today. I wouldn't be at this University, writing this essay, training to be a peer tutor, learning why my childhood was vaguely colonialist. In fact, as much as I make out standard English to be this great evil in my life, I don't advocate that all students from non-traditional backgrounds totally reject it. Standard English is not inherently problematic, it's the way that it's taught. I don't look back on my education and want one that prioritizes my home discourse more. I simply wish I had been given the opportunity to develop a consciousness about my contradictory subject positions. I wish I wasn't taught to see English as a superior language and that I didn't develop such an inferiority complex around speaking and writing in Arabic. I wish I had the consciousness to be able to resolve the dissonance between those two conflicting identities.

It wasn't until college that I developed that exact consciousness. My First Year Writing Class was the first time that I was encouraged to interrogate the different discourses and subject positions I had available to me to write in. Our teacher required us to question why we wrote in standard English. For our essays, we were given the option to pick a mode of writing based on the topic and audience assigned to us. If we wanted to write in a wholly academic voice, we had to justify how that voice or discourse was useful in getting across our specific ideas to our specific audience. No discourse, no style of writing was necessarily prioritized over another. It demystified writing for me. I understood the value of writing in certain voices where as previously I had been taught to write in one form solely because "it was better this way".

Moreover, it was the first time writing and literature had been framed as a way to engage with the world as I lived in it. For an alarmingly large part of my life, I genuinely hated reading and writing because it truly felt like the things we read mattered solely because they belonged to an arbitrarily decided on canon of white, Western authors. Discussions in high school were always nudged to a "universal truth" that 9/10 times did not apply to me. I wrote my essays on theses that I did not believe in. I received and reproduced what I thought my teachers wanted to hear. My college writing class was "problem-posing" (Friere 83). In discussions, we were encouraged to put the pieces we read in conversation with our own experiences and use them to think critically about how we lived in the world. We were allowed to come to our own conclusions. Our teacher rarely felt like a higher authority, but an equal member of our conversations. The essays we wrote were based on these discussions and thus meant to be an interrogation of our lived experiences.

Two essays I wrote stand out in my mind as indicative of this. The first compared two short stories to analyze how the narrators of those stories resolved dichotomous images of their mothers. I ended up framing that essay around my own relationship with my mother and by the end of it I came to a conclusion about our relationship I never would have thought of otherwise. I picked up the phone and called her right after I hit submit. The second was a geobiography I wrote about my village, Al-Jalamah. It was the first time I had ever (successfully) written about Palestine in an academic setting. It made me feel like I belonged in that classroom, in this symbolic space I had been chasing affirmation from since I was a child. That essay helped me work through a lot of the dissonance between my identities as Palestinian and American, and the obligations I felt to both of those worlds. I no longer viewed my home and academic discourses as being in opposition.

When I no longer saw my home and academic discourses as dichotomous it reframed my outlook on writing as a whole. All of a sudden writing presented a space of resistance for me. It went from being a reproduction of the dominant thought forced on me to a questioning of that thought. This is what compels me to write now. I don't see my reality as static, but something I can constantly shape via my writing. My thoughts and my voice (both written and audible) have meaning because they allow me to take action within my world.

I want to be a peer tutor because it took me 17 years to start doing the work to decolonize my mindset around writing. I encounter a lot of multilingual students within the center who share the experiences of my childhood. They have had this "absolute ignorance" projected on them by the university or other academic spaces and anxiously want to master English even at the cost of erasing their voice within their writing. It's my job to give them the middle-ground I didn't feel I had: meet their needs while allowing them to interrogate the cost and benefits of the different discourses available to them. How we teach English within the center is more than about improving a grade. Educational equity is a human right and we have to approach it as such.

## Works Cited

Freire, Pablo. *Pedagogy of the Oppressed.* 30th Anniversary edition th ed., 1970.

# Excellence in Upper-Level Writing (Humanities)

## A Second Exile:
## Mario Benedetti's Absence in English
by Davis Boos
*From COMPLIT 322: Translated Wor(l)ds*
*Nominated by Marlon James Sales*

One of the challenges of scholarly writing in Translation Studies (TS) ensues from a need to strike a healthy balance between theory and praxis, between source and target, between the translator and the translated. As one recent edited monograph boldly states, TS is a rare discipline in the humanities where scholars are generally practitioners themselves. TS scholars are tasked to reflect on their choices as translators, or meditate on another translator's creative practice, tacitly comparing it to their own. Because of the wide array of texts that can potentially be translated, TS scholars are likewise expected to have a firm grasp of genres and registers, a knowledge of languages and dialects, an understanding of the subject matter of the text, and a readiness to conduct research to fill in the gaps. Davis Boos's essay is a clear example of how elegantly these expectations can be achieved. Upon translating two short stories by the revered Uruguayan writer Mario Benedetti, Davis set out to evaluate his translation strategy, initially on the basis of his linguistic choices. How would Uruguayan Spanish look like in an English-language translation? How could references be explicitated without being too pedantic? How should realia be made known to a new readership? It soon became evident that these choices were addressing broader cultural concerns. From here emerged a reflective piece on linguistic exile, which approaches Benedetti's situatedness in a specific reading culture as a function of translation. Davis's maturity as a writer is seen in his acknowledgment of his ethical commitments to the translation process, well as in his consistent self-critique, which foregrounds the discontents of that inevitable tug and pull that all translators experience.

-- *Marlon James Sales*

# A Second Exile:
# Mario Benedetti's Absence in English

### Introduction

Knowledge no longer atrophies with time. The amount of information we collect and possess is staggering. If nothing goes unrecorded, it is easy to think that history will cease to be unclear. There is video, in color and with sound, of nearly every historical event of the last two decades. Libraries, no matter how large, can be indexed in seconds from any computer in the world. If the researcher of the future has sufficient patience and will, it seems that the facts of our present cannot elude them.

But the historian will not die. The abundance of information we accrue daily will need to be sorted. The historian will still need to connect the dots and describe the lines between them. They will find what is valuable in what we mindlessly store away for them. And to do so, they must be able to hear the voices of the time in which they focus. They must be able to access the perspectives of those who recorded what happened, how it happened and how it changed them. And they must do so broadly; they must cast the widest net possible. For a history is the unification of disparate perspectives: what can now be called History in the singular was once a multitude of outlooks belonging to as many individuals living distinct lives, each construed differently. To not include as many of these realities as possible is to preclude the creation of a complete, and one could go on to argue accurate, history. To leave out a perspective is to leave the depiction of our past lacking.

I write in, as the placard at the door told me, the fourth largest Asian Studies library in North America. There is no doubt that close at hand there are well constructed articles describing political events crucial to the development of a contemporary China, tragic poetry conveying the hardships of a farmer in the west who was forgotten in the rising global tide. But I am no closer to these perspectives, this information, than I was before entering this building today.

The Chinese characters elude me. These perspectives preserved cannot aide me in shining a light on the past or present. Here, the translator shoulders the burden of keeping alive a complete past. They have the power to repatriate a reader from an obscure exile borne not out of spatial but linguistic separation, for those pages are absent even as I hold them in my hands. Inside this building, if I move from the Asia library to another, walking from shelf to shelf, language to language, I will fall in and out of my exile. Everyone here does the same. Suddenly and often, a great but invisible void opens up between us and the texts at our flanks.

Among these shelves, one will find the work of Mario Benedetti. Despite winning a suite of literary prizes and holding several honorary doctorate degrees, Benedetti's voice can not be heard outside the Spanish-speaking world. But the whims of translation are not the first power to force him into exile. In the late 20th century, a brutal dictatorship kept him separated from his home of Uruguay for twelve years. He is best known for his stories and poetry that express and process the bitter trauma, sorrow and helplessness that came from that experience. Keeping this perspective alive and ceasing his second estrangement was my initial motivation for the translation. But beyond this academic aim, it became apparent that his work has a clear connection to our present.

It is obvious that those exiled are physically separated from their homeland, but Benedetti introduced to me the idea that one's conception of this homeland remains static. The country that the exile flees from will continue to change, but they will know it only as it was on the day of their departure. They are left with a memory that fails to represent reality. The sense of estrangement this phenomenon produces is immense. Benedetti captures it here in one of his poems, *Eso dicen* [They Say] (1984, 19):

| Eso dicen | [They say |
|---|---|
| que al cabo de diez años | that after ten years |
| todo ha cambiado | everything has changed |
| allá | there |
| | |
| dicen | Saying |
| que la avenida está sin árboles | that the avenue is without trees |
| y no soy quién para ponerlo en duda | and I'm not one to doubt it |
| | |
| ¿acaso yo no estoy sin árboles | Perhaps I am not without the trees |
| que según dicen | that to them |
| ya no están? | are no longer there?][1] |

Can this one perspective serve to represent all those that have been forced to flee their homeland? No. The picture remains incomplete. But it is improved by a degree. And we are reminded that the other perspectives in the world exist yet unheard. Today, fifty years after Benedetti's first exile, Latin Americans are leaving their countries in alarmingly large numbers, and the issue is at the forefront of American political rhetoric. They are similar in experience with Benedetti, all but forced to leave a country in turmoil and thereby subject to tremendous alienation. One is compelled to think of this when reading Benedetti's work today. Next decade's reader will be reminded of something now unknown. And Benedetti's work will remain a part of history that can ground our understanding of the variety of presents we are faced with. I am convinced there will be a perennial role for Benedetti's portrayal of humanity, and so here it will be translated. And in order to fully understand that translation, the Uruguay of that era needs to first be understood.

## The Making of an Author: Benedetti's Political Past

For much of Latin America, the second half of the twentieth century mirrors the brutal and inhumane patterns of colonialism from which the continent had only recently escaped. This is especially true for the three countries that compose the region known as the Southern Cone—Argentina, Uruguay and Chile. The Cone is most famous for the dictators that came to power there during the Cold War period. Young democracy gave way to military control, kidnappings,

---

[1] Unless otherwise specified, all tranlations in this text are my own.

tourture, arbitrary imprisonment, and the absence of free expression. In Uruguay, the military backed dictatorship which came to power in 1973 would precipitate the exile of close to 380,000 people or fourteen percent of the population (Schelotto 2015, 2-3).

Before this national tragedy, a child named Mario was born in the small town of Paso de los Toros on September 13, 1920. It was a Monday. He moved to the capital city of Montevideo at the age of four and grew up there. As a teenager he read an eclectic mix of authors: Chekhov, Maupassant, Hemingway, Proust, Quiroga and Svevo. He would live in Argentina for a decade as a young man before moving back to Montevideo. There he would marry Luz López Alegre in 1946, the year after publishing his first collection of poetry. Benedetti went on to publish six works in a variety of genres over the next decade while also working for the magazine *Número*. To make ends meet he worked where he could, anything from cashier to stenographer (Flores 1992, 93-96).

In the mid-50s he began as a serious contributor to and editor of the weekly newspaper *Marcha*, and his involvement in the politics of the country intensified greatly. Always on the Left, he became increasingly socialist as the years went on, seeming to find inspiration in Cuba's revolution (Gregory 2008, 25). He was a minor candidate, but a candidate nonetheless, for the socialist party in the 1962 elections. He also played a major role in the political group *El Movimiento de Independientes 26 de Marzo* [The March 26th Independence Movement; M26 hereafter], helping to found and lead the organization (Gregory 2008, 27). M26 would then go on to join *Frente Amplio* [Broad Front], a coalition of left wing parties designed to consolidate political control (Arregui 2016, 16-17). Such a curriculum vitae all but painted a target on his back for the fascists accumulating power and control in the country. He had to choose between imprisonment, torture and possible death in Uruguay or a lonely exile abroad when the dictatorship began in 1973.

He chose exile. He first found refuge close to home in Argentina, but after two short years the government there was also engulfed in a military dictatorship;

he was forced to move on to Lima, Peru. A year later, in 1976, he moved to Cuba and stayed there in Havana for seven years. He spent the last two years of his exile in Madrid before finally returning to Uruguay with the restoration of Democracy in 1985 (Wilson 2010, 193-194). This exile would come to define the man and his work.

As such, I translated two stories that deal directly with the contours of exile: *Geografías* [Geographies] and *De puro distraído* [Out of Pure Distraction]. Both pieces are a part of a collection also titled *Geografías* that was published in 1984 on the eve of Benedetti's return to Montevideo. It includes fourteen short stories interspersed with poetry, all focused sharply on the experience of exile. The pieces I have chosen are emblematic of Benedetti's experience and showcase two ostensibly disjoint accounts of the exiled. But in reality they do not represent mutually exclusive experiences. Rather, they are different phases of and reactions to such a prolonged and pervasive trauma.

## How (and why) Benedetti Came to be in English

When I began to translate these texts, my principal consideration was how they were intended to interact with the reader. Katharina Reiß was a pioneer in defining functions a text may serve (Munday 2016, 113-118). Generally, poems and literary short stories would be almost purely expressive texts concerned with nothing but conveying the emotion of the reader. However, these works, in the time of their creation, served a distinctly operative function at par with that of their expressive intentions. That is, they were written to stir emotional and political aspirations in their readers, to evoke the sorrow of the many exiled but then transform it into action against the political regime which inflicted so much pain. Benedetti speaks on the nature of this kind of writing in the prologue to his collection of fiction *Letras de emergencia* [Writings for an Emergency],

> Creo que este libro es literatura, pero de emergencia; es decir, directamente motivada por la coyuntura, y también claramente destinada a desempeñar una función social o política, pero no como **panfleto** sino como **literatura** (Benedetti 1978, 9; emphasis in the original).

[I believe that this book is a piece of literature, but it's made for a state of emergency. That is, it's directly motivated by the situation and also is clearly intended to achieve social and political aims but not as a **pamphlet**. Instead, it does so as **literature**.]

The author himself clearly explains he had social and political aims, even in his creative work.

However this operative function has transformed into an informative one today—it is no longer possible to take action against the Uruguayan military regime. The dictator is dead. Therefore, this text serves to explain and retell the horrible history that those who were exiled lived through. Given these aims, it was imperative for this translation that moments where the pain of exile manifest were preserved and emphasized as much as is possible, even at the expense of artistic expression or beauty in form. The translation problems and compromises that come along with this mindset, when explained, are able to yield a richer reading of both the source text (ST hereafter) and the target text (TT hereafter).

## Geografías/Geographies

Even before this ST is subjected to a formal translation, it is replete with foreign elements and therefore pre-existing forms of translation. Benedetti retained many titles and phrases in languages other than the text's principal language of Spanish to remind the reader of the characters' physical exile in the narrative. While I reiterated these devices of estrangement conceived by Benedetti, the majority of the translation (namely, the first three quarters) is largely domesticated. This was a decision founded on a consideration of the likely target audience for these translated stories. This conceived audience could be described as having academic tendencies but falling far short of expertise on the subject. An individual who seriously researches the specific field of Latin American exile would almost certainly have the ability to read the ST in Spanish, rendering my translation unimportant for them. However, I do not see this work as intended for the complete opposite side of the spectrum either; it is not light reading. This is a work that elaborates on painful trauma through a somewhat inaccessible streamof-consciousness style. In accordance with Vermeer's Skopos theory, and more specifically, the coherence rule, which posits that, "[t]he TT must be translated in such a way that makes sense for the TT receivers, given their circumstances, knowledge and needs" (Munday 2016, 128), I decided that a TT filled with an excessive amount of foreign elements or one that contained highly specific foreign elements would strip it of important meaning rather than foster a more complete picture of the interplay between the different cultures at hand.

There are two very clear manifestations of this strategy in the translation among the many smaller details. The first is centered on the word *picana*. This word translates to cattle prod, and in many circumstances this is a perfectly acceptable translation. But within the context of Southern Cone dictatorships, this word has much darker and serious connotations. Such a device was commonly used in that region to brutally torture prisoners with an electrical current. Once that is known, it is obvious that a literal translation would not suffice to convey the meaning imbued in the ST. Further, the sucessful translation of this word is imparative to the sucess of the work as a whole; the juxtaposition and mutual exclusivity of the mental pain of exile and the physical pain of torture is central to *Geografías*. To convey the appropriate meaning, I employed a dynamic translation strategy. The TT thus reads, "...as if she came from an evening of playing canasta or from a beach in the mederterrianan, not from darkened cells and broken fingers and cattle prods on the other side of the Atlantic." The literal translation appears, but a phrase describing the connotation it carries—torture and deprivation— accompines it. The ST makes no mention of darkened cells or broken fingers, but they are included in the TT to signify that the "cattle prod" is not an agricultural instrument here. While the addition is not nearly as elegant or succinct as using a single word, the aesthetic loss is justified by a cross-cultural clarity in the TT. Now a reader unfamiliar with this niche torutre device can still understand that the character was subjected to brutal and inhumane captivity.

The second large example of explicitation is found in the following portion of the TT: "For example? Dieciocho de Julio no longer has trees. **Did you**

**know that there is no longer shade to walk beneath on that long avenue in the heart of our city?** Ah." The bolded section of my translation is an addition made for the TT. This was done because someone unfamiliar with Montevideo would not recognize "Dieciocho de Julio" as major thoroughfare in the city. This passage describes the mutilation of an iconic city landmark, a massive change to the city that Roberto, the narrator from Montevideo, was not aware of until that moment. The trees missing from the street would be somewhat equivalent to a portion of Central Park being clear cut, and a reader unfamiliar with Montevideo could not know this degree of importance without added explanation. Now it is clear that the characters are discussing an avenue and that it is an important or at least prominent feature in the center of Montevideo. While this addition does not perfectly and explicitly explain what Dieceocho de Julio signifies for the characters or any Uruguayan in exile, I did not want my explanation to be excessive. Something akin to the style of a footnote would certainly be out of place in a short story. This addition gives enough information so the reader can have a clearer understanding of what is being described but avoids belaboring the explanation to a point where the narrative is disrupted.

The two instances described above detail how domestication of the ST was necessary for the audience's comprehension of crucial points made within *Geografías*. There are foreign elements in the translation, but they do not pose serious obstacles to the communicative power of the TT. For any reader with a small amount of patience and willingness to embrace unfamiliarity in a text, these foreignizing elements serve as reminders that the text is a translation and that it was written in a setting foreign to the author himself. Names and terms of endearment in Spanish tended to be retained in the TT (Gaucho, Salvo, Porteña, Viejo) and all the French (Quartier, Passez Pietons, Toilette) and German (Kaputt) used by Benedetti in the ST remained in the TT. The meanings of these words are not crucial to the narrative or themes of the text, and therefore can be left in a language other than English without concern of confusing the reader.

That being said, the comments above on foreign elements only hold true until the final paragraph of the work—this final segment of the TT is replete with zero translation. Upon first glance, this sudden and drastic change in translation strategy may seem impulsive and unfounded. However, this is a text principally concerned with estrangement, that of the narrator from his homeland. Such a detail presents a great opportunity for translation to increase the thematic power of the story. Translation, or its absence, can exile the reader from the text just as the characters are exiled from their home.

The bulk of this story takes place in a cafe where the characters play a game in which details of Uruguay are recalled. This game is a coping mechanism constructed around the characters' nostalgia for home. It supports and maintains the illusion that they are not strangers to their country, that they are capable of returning to the Uruguay that they remember. Likewise, the reader, in this section of the TT, is offered the illusion, through domestication, that the text he or she reads was written in English. The explanations and grammar structures here attempt to shield the reader from estrangement, just as the game of geographies is an attempt to shield the characters from estrangement. But by the end of this story, the illusion of the geographies collapses for the narrator, and Delia's character forces him to realize the extent and irreparability of his status as an exile, that he is hopelessly detached from Uruguay. He is a stranger to his home. Therefore, to amplify this essential theme present in the ST, the reader, in this section, is placed in a linguistic exile through zero translation. The reader becomes a stranger to the text he or she has become comfortable with. Suddenly, English gives way to Spanish, and crossing the boundary into an unknown language represents the pinnacle of incomprehension. This happens in lockstep with Roberto confronting the unintelligibility of his Uruguay. He know longer understands a place he once knew just as the reader can no longer understand a text they had just read without issue. The Spanish in the TT replicates the effect of the physical distance in Roberto's exile. Both elements, the physical separation from Uruguay and the use of Spanish, are means to the same end, for in each case the individual is removed and precluded from accessing knowledge. Within the story, Roberto is unable to know what changes have been wrought in Uruguay. Outside the story, the reader is no longer able to know what Benedetti describes or the characters say. While zero translation may not convey the same emotional pain of exile, it can certainly convey the same frustration that one feels in being cut off from an entire reality, and therefore allows the reader to connect intimately with the protagonist.

This intimate connection forged between reader and protagonist, and by extension reader and author, is an important to notice instance of the act of translation adding to and improving on elements of the ST. In fact, it does so in a way that only translation can. Although a translation's function of making a work accessible to a wider audience is certainly essential, important and the basis of the discipline, it is not a function that stands alone. Here we see that translation is a creative endeavour in and of itself. It is a process by which elements are both uncovered from and added to a text. The result is something altogether new which is capable of providing its own novel insight. Translation is not, as many may think, a process through which a work is disfigured to yield a sad replacement for the original.

## De puro distraído/Out of Pure Distraction

The second story translated, *De puro distaído* [Out of pure distraction], is remarkably different than *Geografías*. Witin *De puro distraído*, there is no harkening back to the past or crippling nostalgia; rather, exile is met with extreme detachment. Few places are named, and it is never specifically said that the protagonist is a Uruguayan exile; Benedetti writes:

> Así como había vagado por las calles y los caminos de su tierra, empezó a vagar por los países, las fronteras y los mares. Era terriblemente distraído. A menudo no sabía en qué ciudad se encontraba, pero no por eso se decidía a preguntar (Benedetti 1984, 72).

> [Just as he had roamed the streets and roads of his own nation, he began to drift through countries, borders and seas. He was terribly distracted. He often did not know which city he found himself in, but he decided not to question this.]

The protagonist in exile is so fundamentally lost, he seems to have forgotten his trauma.

Being that foreign elements are intentionally subdued, a predominantly dynamic translation strategy, where cultural and linguistic character from the ST do not often manifest in the TT, was employed. Benedetti is attempting to convey a sense of detachment and distractedness from place. An attempt to foreignize this text would undercut that purpose and yield a TT out of accordance with the theme of the ST. The reader, just as the protagonist is, should be unaware of specific locations and cultures, not reminded of them. While I support the idea of showcasing foreign elements in a TT to remind the reader that they have been presented a text in translation, I do not think such a strategy should be applied ubiquitously. Foreignizing for the sake of foreignizing—that is, without a well-reasoned purpose or to improve understanding—toes the line of exoticization and may be jarring, counterproductive or questionable for readers of the TT. In this translation of *De puro distraído*, the reader will find no Spanish, and only several foreign names that are also present in the ST. Grammar structures and idioms will be familiar to the English speaker. Compared to *Geografías*, this is quite a straightforward translation; there were no large hurdles in understanding or conveyance to overcome. It mostly dealt in the realm of denotation rather than connotation.

The process of creating this TT served to highlight the fluid reality of translation. When juxtaposed with my experience translating *Geografías*, it was made clear that the ST and its aim ought to dictate the terms of the translation, and that different texts, or even different portions in the same text, will be best served by different and seemingly incompatible strategies. The great struggle of translation is that between preserving the foreign and suppressing it. In order to achieve the comprehension which I exalted at the beginning of this commentary, foreignness must be erased. The reader must cease to be a stranger. But if one goes too far, the reader will fail to comprehend the context and culture of the work's origins. No one can say where to draw this line. Certainly it is not static. So the translator must not blindly transcribe but carefully listen when they both create and preside over the relationship between source and target texts. For they hold great power as the fiduciary of the once provincial knowledge they strive to spread more broadly in this world.

References

Arregui, Roque. 2016. *Historia del Frente Amplio: 45 años en los nacional y en Soriano*. Montevideo: Editorial Fin de Siglo.

Benedetti, Mario. 1978. *Letras de Emergencia*. México : Editorial Nueva Imagen. Benedetti, Mario. 1984. *Geografías*. Madrid : Alfaguara

Chasteen, John Charles. 2016. *Born in Blood and Fire: A Concise History of Latin America*. New York: W.W. Norton & Company.

Fernández, Wilson. 2010. "Mario Benedetti: Biografía Y Poemas." *Cadernos PROLAM/USP 9*, no. 16: 192-203. doi:10.11606/issn.1676-6288. prolam.2010.82413.

Flores, Angel. 1992. *Spanish American Authors : The Twentieth Century*. New York: H.W. Wilson.

Gregory, Stephen. 2008. "The Road or the Inn? Mario Benedetti as Activist and *El Movimiento de Independientes 26 de Marzo*." Journal of Iberian and Latin American Research, 14:1: 25-47. https://doi-org.proxy.lib. umich.edu/10.1080/13260219.2008.9649892

Magdalena Schelotto. 2015. "La Dictadura Cívico-Militar Uruguaya (1973-1985): La Construcción de La Noción de Víctima y La Figura Del Exiliado En El Uruguay Post-Dictatorial." *Nuevo Mundo—Mundos Nuevos*. doi:10.4000/nuevomundo.67888.

Munday, Jeremy. 2016. *Introducing Translation Studies : Theories and Applications*. London: Routledge. Accessed December 1, 2019. ProQuest Ebook Central.

www.ingramcontent.com/pod-product-compliance
Lightning Source LLC
LaVergne TN
LVHW051159080426
835508LV00021B/2700